"Art, when inspired with love, leads to higher realms. Love art and that art will open for you the inner life."
~Meher Baba

VITRUVIAN LENS

Edition 6
Winter 2014
Editor E. Gibbons
Art Historian Grady Harp
Copy Editor Paul Rybarczyk & Grady Harp
Layout, Design, Production E. Gibbons
Design Consultant Dana Ranning
Publisher Firehouse Publishing

ISBN-10: 1940290376
ISBN-13: 978-1-940290-37-9

Information: *Vitruvian Lens* was founded in 2013, www.VitruvianLens.com, produced by Firehouse Publishing.
Availablility: Please visit www.VitruvianLens.com for the most current pricing, store locations, and general information on eBooks once available. For questions, please e-mail LOVSART@gmail.com or call 609-298-3742. Price is subject to change without notification.
Submissions: *Vitruvian Lens* considers submissions of artists and writers. Contact LOVSART@gmail.com, subject "V.L. Submission," for additional information.
Advertising: For advertising rates, wholesale bulk pricing, and other information, LOVSART@gmail.com.
Distribution: Online through our website www.VitruvianLens.com. For information e-mail LOVSART@gmail.com.
Printing: Published by Firehouse Publishing, headquartered at 8 Walnut Street, Bordentown, NJ 08505.

© 2014 by Firehouse Publishing and Firehouse Gallery. All rights reserved. No part of this book may be reproduced without the express consent of Firehouse Publishing, Firehouse Gallery, and its owner, E. Gibbons.

Important Disclaimer: No assumptions should be made about the gender or sexuality of any artist included in this book. Though all of the artists dedicate a significant portion of their portfolio to the classical male form, they are equally adept in other subjects as well. If you see something you'd like to purchase, contact the artist directly.

Right: Lakolak, *Oceanos in Forest Zone,* 2013
Cover: marc antonio, *cascata III,* 2011
Rear Cover: Yechiely, *Eros,* 2013

CONTENTS

Yechiely 6

18 Lakolak

Louis-Jean Baptiste Igout 30
By Grady Harp

40 Klimov

50 marc antonio™

Federico 62

72 Vintage Collection

DIRECTORY 84

GUY YECHIELY

Vitruvian Lens: Please tell us about yourself.
Guy Yechiely: I'm living and working in Tel Aviv, Israel. I was born in 1982 in Haifa Israel, grew up in a northern town named Karmiel. When I was eighteen I joined the army and served for four years as an artillery officer.

After the army I studied photography in the Bezalel academy of art and design in Jerusalem. Today I live and work in Tel Aviv, and one can see that I'm attracted to the classical, beautiful, aesthetic, and the formal in photography, mostly focusing on directing situations and the use artificial light in order to create a dramatic moment and highlighting it. My work connects with Western art in the eighteenth and ninteenth centuries, with neo-classical painters like Jean Auguste Dominique Ingres, Jacques-Louis David, and other cultural icons. I am trying to capture different aspects, and dealing complicated subjects, like orientalism, politics, and Middle Eastern culture, with a unique approach.

V.L.: What is it about your approach that makes your work unique?
G.Y.: I mostly direct situations, and try to deal with historical and political issues with a modern perspective. One can observe in my pictures include symbols connected to the present day.

In my photos you can find a lot of references to the bible, to past paintings, and beliefs of political issues—sometimes I'm a bit cynical about in my approach to these issues.

V.L.: You have a very powerful portfolio; can you explain your imagery a bit for us?
G.Y.: In Greek mythology, Eros is the god of love and of sexual desire. In contrast, Thanatos is the personification of death. Both are represented in art as attractive young men.

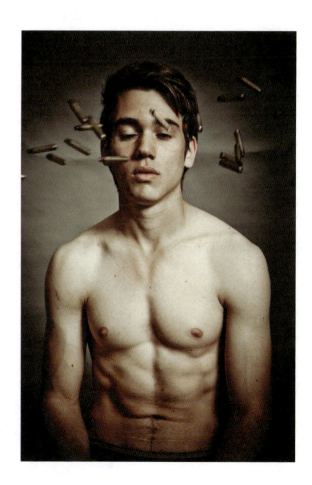

Left: Yechiely, *Swamps 345,* 2013
Right: Yechiely, *Eros,* 2013

Above: Yechiely, *Groundsels Field*, 2013   Right: Yechiely, *Swamps 148*, 2013

According to Freud's psychoanalytic theory, man's two main impulses are Eros–the sex drive and the representation of life, as opposed to Thanatos–the fate of death and the aggression drive. These two impulses are in constant conflict.

In this project I combined the two various aspects with a modern, more local view: The seventeen and eighteen year old boys represent the Eros, young, beautiful, but naive–a step away from joining the military for three years, which is a mandatory in Israel. The military represents Thanatos, with its main purpose of violence, aggression, and destruction. It takes those young naive boys (Eros) and fills them with new ideals; the urge for self-destruction.

The pictures are full of cultural, national and international icons. For example, *The Crying Soldier* stands on a dramatic yellowish ground, crying, next to a burned down house maybe on a battle field. It makes the viewer thinks, why does he cry? What's about? Where is he? The iconic picture is taken from the drawings of *Niños Llorando* by Bruno Amadio which were very popular in Israel 80's.

The Victim photo is dark, gloomy, and showing a man with a weapon raising the head of another man–both unknown, like an image of Greek men fight or a biblical scene, but also an icon of what we see in the media every day–a struggle that ends with an unknown man showing the body of his victim. *The Wounded Soldier* is carried by another soldier, walking on a Groundsel field, which grows everywhere in Israel and familiar in some army songs.

V.L.: Do you have a humorous experience you can share related to your work?

G.Y.: Yes, when I shot the picture *The Victim*, I asked my models to change clothes and do different poses for the camera. We were shooting next to a central town in Israel and I saw a man standing on a small hill next to us, watching and speaking on the phone. After five minutes a police car rushed and stopped right next to the photo-shoot with two policemen running towards me with pistols in their hands, I explained them the situation and told them, that yes, it a bit weird to see half naked soldiers running around, but they understood, laughed, and it was a very funny experience.

V.L.: What do you hope for the future of your work? What goals have you set?

G.Y.: Well, my main goal is to be represented in a well-known gallery and my dream is to have exhibitions around the world. I noticed that the art world is full of politics and favoritism but I feel my work is being well received and I really believe in it.

V.L.: How has your style developed?

G.Y.: I like movies. I like to "cut" amazing frames in my mind, examine them, explore them, and understand what's making them so special. I can tell you about a recent example from the movie *Django Unchained*, there is a short scene where blood is spilled on a cotton field, I think that image is so dramatic and amazingly made, an image that expands your eyes, and makes you think.

I also, of course, am very attracted to Greek and Roman sculptures, history, and empires. I also adore the neo-classical painters and ultra-realist art.

V.L.: Tell me something people might not know about you or your work?

G.Y.: I want people to think, to ask questions, to be upset, or just have an opinion about my work. I don't care if they will like it or not. The opinion is what matters. I want people to explore and understand what I want to show them, I'm trying to bring a story to life,

Yechiely, *Swamps 134*, (cropped) 2013

and behind it there are a lot of issues hiding.

V.L.: Who would be your inspirations?
G.Y.: Photographers like Helmut Newton, Richard Avadon, David LaChapelle, and more. Locally would be Adi Nes. I am very inspired by painters as Jean August Dominiq Ingres, Jean-Léon Gérôme, Jacque Louis David, and the Greek and Roman sculptures from ancient times.

V.L.: Where do you find your models?
G.Y.: I mostly ask people I find interesting to come and model for me. I don't ask for professional models. I like when people are true and less "trying to be models" for the photo.

V.L.: Tell us about your very first exhibition.
G.Y.: My first exhibition was in the Bezalel Academy and I was very nervous and excited. I created an exhibition about orientalism and I not only hung pictures on the wall, I also put huge Persian carpets on the floor, and made some video-art with great sound. People who came in could enjoy a whole experience, not just pictures on a wall.

V.L.: When did you know you wanted to be a photographer/artist?
G.Y.: I always knew. It was burning in me, and everybody that remembers me young always noticed me going around with a camera.
I think they weren't shocked when I went to study at the art academy.

V.L.: Can you live off your work yet?
G.Y.: I think the main issue, as an artist, is to understand—at least In the near future—that you cannot live on that. You also know that you do art, not for the sale sake, but for your own sake. If it burns in you, you just must do it, and not worry about sales. Of cause I would be very happy to make a living from it, and sell as much as I can, but the most important thing is that people will enjoy my pictures and find them interesting

Yechiely, *Swamps 60*, (cropped) 2013

Yechiely, *Swamps 80*, (cropped) 2013

Photography is an expensive business so I work as an advertising manager in a jewelry company, and use that money to spend on my art.

V.L.: What subject is the most challenging for you as an artist to capture?
G.Y.: I think that the most challenging for me is to find the right image that will reflect all what I feel and see inside of it. The saying *"a picture is worth a thousand words"* is very true, and to make that kind of picture is a real challenge.

For more information aboug Guy, please visit:
facebook.com/guyyechielyart
www.guyyechiely.com
or Guy Yechiely (facebook)
or Email: Guytlv@gmail.com

Above: Yechiely, *The Crying Soldier*, 2014

Below: Yechiely, *The Victim*, 2014

Above: Yechiely, *The Awakening*, 2013 Below: Yechiely, Swamps 78, 2013

Above: Yechiely, *Swamps 115*, 2013

Below: Yechiely, *Swamps 77*, 2013

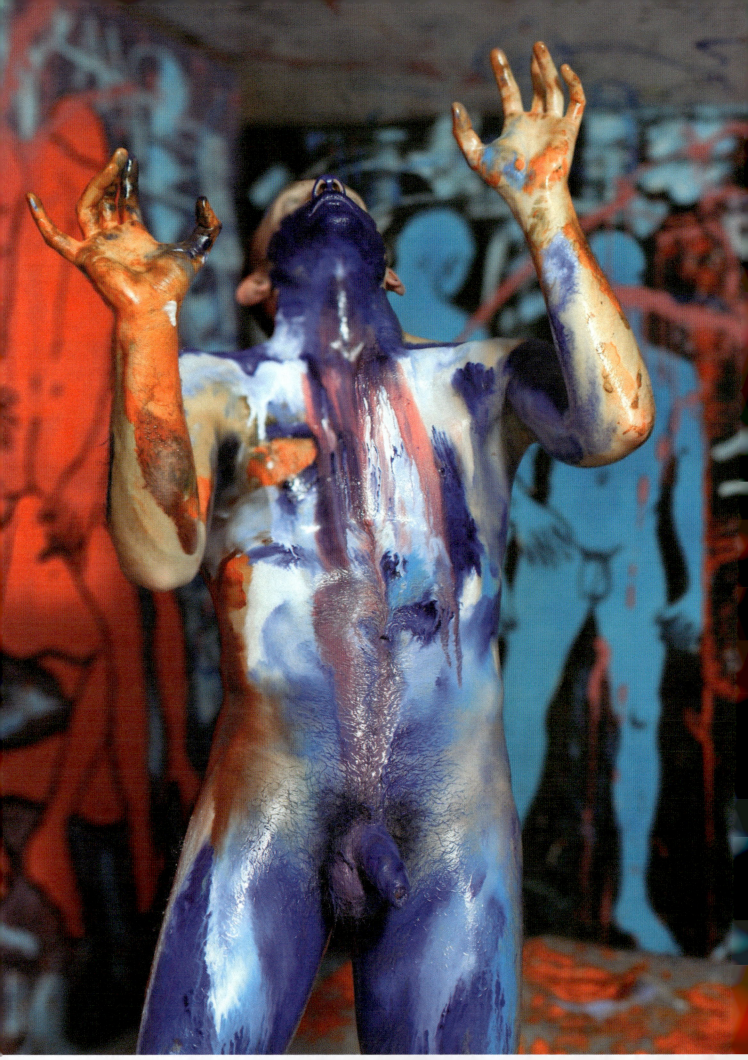

KARL LAKOLAK

Karl Lakolak, and his alter ego *Meton Atopik,* have always been drawing the human body, especially the male body. It was like he was searching for his own image in a fantasmatic alter ego or mirror. He used to draw the nude bodies of his young friends, his models, those of ancient sculptures and paintings. The body soon became a body of supernatural temptation, of simulacrum, stronger than truth.

Karl has been discovering the virtues of the nude by studiously copying the naked Apollo Belvedere found in his history books. He understood very early that the erotic magic and bewitchment generated by the representation of the fantasized body is a spiritual journey.

Over Time, Karl has been building multiple identities, as he plays *the art game*. The painting he'd dreamt about for so long became "alive." His large size canvases, decorative ornaments, and scenery are displayed on each wall, floor, and ceiling of the studio—a small renovated theatre. Karl creates fictions and museum stories in which naked and painted bodies wander while being filmed and photographed.

Karl often went to the Louvre museum in his youth to copy works of art. Before becoming photographer and videographer, he was interested in painting and drawing. He is currently focused on art history at Paris 1 University.

Vitruvian Lens: Why do you include more male figures in your portfolio?

Karl Lakolak: This is very simple to answer, I think many artists are searching for their own image by drawing and photographing the human body, and many artist speak of their affects and love passions. So I'm naturally interested in narcissistic and homoerotic questions. What is really important for me is to speak about desire.

Above: Lakolak, *Blue Standing Man*, 2014
Left: Lakolak, *Waterfall on Groove Thang*, 2014

Lakolak, *Lying in Forest Zone*, 2014

V.L.: What is it about your work or approach that you feel is unique?
K.L.: That is not so easy to answer, perhaps an overdose of romantically but wild vision of the body, focused with a high emotionally tone: a mix of violence and emotional tone in a duality world, as if David Hamilton has been merged with Robert Mapplethorpe.

V.L.: Have you encountered any issues with having the male figure in your work?
K.L.: Though a wind of freedom blows in occidental democracy with homoeroticism and minority sexualities, due to the heroic and courageous gay activists, especially in early America, the world is still hetero sexist or at least dominated by a straight normative way of life.

Lakolak, *Mathieu Paint Worker*, 2013

For many people, you're not entirely a good citizen if you choose to focus on homoerotic figures, while the female nude is still a must in our culture! Curiously, the male nude body became scandalous again, as if the penis was charged with problematic acceptance.

V.L.: Do you see a change in the acceptance of the male figure as subject?

K.L.: Of course, we're not in the bad old times when Van Gloeden was shunned for his wonderful art! The male figure is joining the female figure in production of sex symbols now; the male is also now the object of desire for everybody!

Lakolak
Divinity in Forest Zone
2013

Lakolak, *Sleeper*, 2014

V.L.: Have you had any unusual experiences with a model or client?

K.L.: Once I was confronted with a gender issue. Often I do casting myself through friends. I met a young man who seemed so nice on facebook and we decided to organize a session—in fact the man was a girl in transition to become a man. What a big surprise and a great moment to converse with her, to speak about her troubles, especially with her parents, her difficulty to live her choice, so I did the job!

V.L.: Are there subjects you are considering for future works you can share?

K.L.: I'm working on performances and short films, always connected to my photographic work. I worked on a video project about love and art, a passionate and candid story between two men, with poetic words, dialog, and voice-over. I try to integrate real life in my fictional living paintings.

V.L.: How do you feel when your work pops up on social websites like Tumblr or Pinterest?

K.L.: In truth I like learning that someone is interested in my work. I think I'm a network artist and sharing is the mover of my creations—the museum network is hugely powerful!

V.L.: If you could own just one work of art, which one would it be?

K.L.: *The Embarkation for Cythera*, 1717, by Jean-Antoine Watteau; though my son has been repeating so many time to me that this piece is highly insipid! It reminds me of the dreamlike magic of a crepuscular world, and the precious and fragility of innocent lovers painted by the Master of the "Fêtes Galantes."

Lakolak, *Lying in Forest Zone*, 2013

Lakolak
Imprint
2014

V.L.: How has your style developed?
K.L.: I've always been interested in drawing the body. When I was twenty, I discovered Leni Riefenstahl's books with photographs of tribes published in 1974 and 1976 as *The Last of the Nuba* and *The People of Kau*. I was so impressed by their tribal body painting traditional practices! At the same time I heard about the performances of French artist Yves Klein, *Anthropometry*. Some works Klein made using naked female models covered in blue paint and dragged across or laid upon canvases to make an image, using the models as living brushes.

More recently I've been watching an excellent documentary about the Vienna Actionist Hermann Nitsch and his *Orgien Mysterien Theater* performances; both ritualistic and existential. The incredible artist is a Master!

V.L.: Tell me something people might not know about you or your work?
K.L.: I humbly think that I'm influenced by paradoxes; the yin and the yang, Dr Jekyll and Mister Hyde; I live with my wife who supports my artwork against all odds; I'm the happy father of a beloved son! I think nobody's perfect.

V.L.: Who would be your inspirations?
K.L.: I've already spoken about Vienna actionists, I'm very fascinated by El Greco and his mesmerizing nude bodies. I often study Delacroix, drawings by Watteau, and copy Velasquez, Rubens, Gustave Moreau, and so many other artists I like! An artist's inspirations changed so much with the availability of the Internet—we are saturated with information and photographs.

V.L.: Where do you find your models?
K.L.: Early, I used to find my actors, dancers, and models in real life, even in the street by calling on some fabulous man wandering down the sidewalk. Networking is actually an easy solution for casting. I'm proud to be requested now by models themselves. As I am constantly working in an emergency environment, I've got a big model address book! One day, I was waiting for two models for a shoot and video tracks, all things were ready, but both were suddenly indisposed. In record time, I found two replacements thanks to my personal network. The film became a little bit different, but I did it!

V.L.: Do you remember the first time you ever sold a work of art, or were published?
K.L.: For me it was very long ago, and it was a painting! Really, I'm so proud when one of my works is collected! I must say I don't work with any art dealer, unfortunately, but I used to sell my works very frequently. The pleasure is even more important when I am published, because a book is like a small museum, a private museum, made for dreaming.

V.L.: When did you know you wanted to be a photographer/artist?
K.L.: Curiously, I've always hoped to be a painter, not a photographer, even less a videographer! I began to photograph about fifteen years ago, but now I'm totally fascinated by this technical way to produce artworks with real bodies! For me it's like camera obscura became a living extension of my drawings.

V.L.: Have you ever been brought to tears in front of a work of art?
K.L.: Yes. I remember my first trip to see an exhibition of Vincent van Gogh when I was fifteen. It came as a real psychological shock for me. Also when I saw *Thatched Cottages at Cordeville, Auvers-sur-Oise (1890)* for the second time at the Musée du jeu de Paume. I was petrified and particularly moved. This painting was like food, a spiritual food, and I understood that day that the world is made to be desired, that art was helping us in this dream, and that without desire, frightened and depressed we become.

V.L.: What subject is the most challenging?
K.L.: Beyond doubt, passion between lovers.

For more information please visit:
www.lakolak.info

Above: Lakolak, *Red Man*, 2011

Right: Lakolak, *Study for Alkyoneus*, 2011

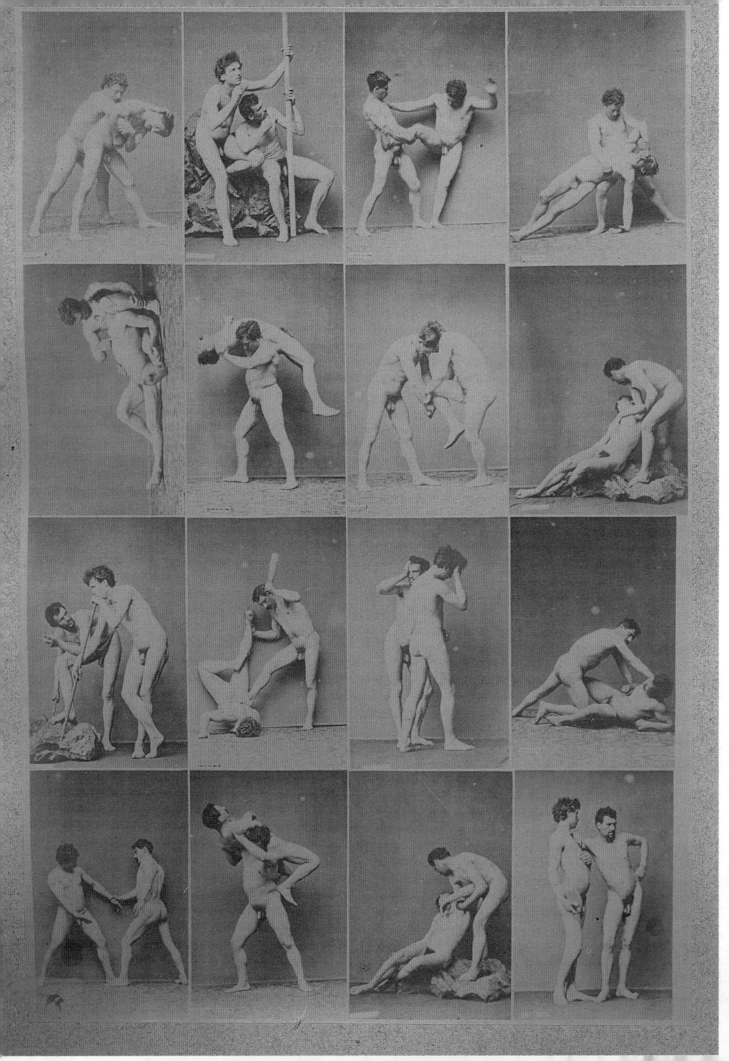

LOUIS-JEAN BAPTISTE IGOUT
By Grady Harp

LOUIS-JEAN BAPTISTE IGOUT
Significant Beginnings
By Grady Harp

The history of photography is a relatively brief one and discovering some of the quiet pioneers of that art form is one of the pleasures of understanding the now appreciated intrinsic role photography has come to play in the creation of art. Not just the large and small, black and white, full color, and computer manipulated images that are considered such a valid art form as *Vitruvian Lens* is proving, but it is the influence of the camera in the development or evolution of painting from the model, now so affordable to all artists who may capture a sitting through a lens to be saved on projection or paper for reference in any hour of the day or night the muse calls, that begs exploring.

The French photographer Louis-Jean Baptiste Igout (1837–1881) is not an immediately recognizable name in art circles, certainly not in the same realm as van Gloeden, Muybridge, Brady, or even Eakins. His goal as a photographer was more that of serving as an adjunct to the painters of his day—and in many circles of academia, to the present. As of 1839 the advent of photography stood at the threshold of an entirely unique role, altering the manner in which art would be perceived subsequently. The ability to capture an image and reproduce it at will jolted the perception of not only artists but also art patrons. Prior to the arrival of the camera, artists depended on earlier painters and sculptors to define the classical figure—for example the nudes of Ingres or the sculptures of ancient Greece. Igout capitalized on the capacity of the camera to arrest motion, to freeze a moment using a live model either nude or draped in various poses.

Once a collection was available, a series of many different models both male and female in varying stances and positions, he marketed these 'ideals' to artists to use in place of mere observation of classical paintings or posing live models. With photography came a renewed interest in the human form, images that ranged from classical poses to pornographic representation of the flesh.

Igout carefully catalogued these images and marketed them as *Académies*–large collections of photographic images both male and female designed to be used as gestational ideas for artists. His models vary from repose to violently contorted poses, works of solo nudes and coupled nudes. Igout's female nudes stand as if sculptures, bodies half veiled, amidst a decadent, classic interior. The passive female figures of these early photos depict in essence the same naked female from decades before.

Igout, *Studio Images*, c. 1880

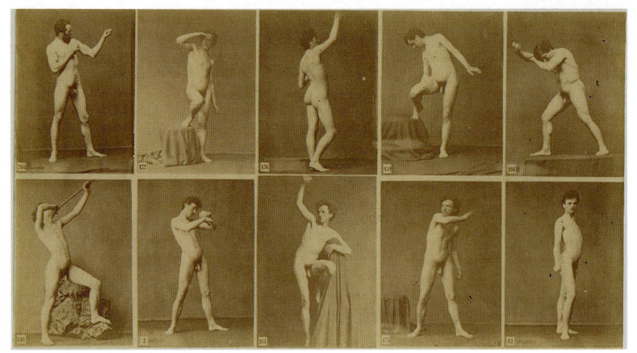

Above and right: Igout, *Studi di Nudo*, c. 1870-80

His usually massively muscular men provided inspiration for the inclusion of mythical heroes in classical canvases as well as passionate introductions to the sensual beginnings of the Pre-Raphaelites.

Working primarily in conjunction with the painters and the Ecole des Beaux-Arts in Paris, he published with the editeur Calavas at 30 boulevard d'Enfer in Paris in the 1870s. Together they created multiple image sheets of four to sixteen single and coupled classical images, nearly forty plates in all (and perhaps many more). Each album intended to represent the contours of the human body (man, woman and child) in a maximum number of possible positions to help the painter represent the body. These he called the academic nude.

Some of Igout's images are highly homoerotic simply by proximity of two male nudes respecting various poses Igout would devise. These images were produced in the time of the Victorian view of sex. While we have scores of photographs of men with men from the American photographers and the privacy of European proponents of male relationships, most of these could be justified as capturing staged moments of brotherly confrères. Yet one of the reasons male friendships were so intense during the 19th and early 20th centuries is that socialization was largely separated by sex: men spent most their time with other men, women with other women. It wasn't until the mid portion of the twentieth century that some psychologists theorized that gender-segregated socialization spurred homosexuality, and as cultural mores changed in general, snapshots of only men together were supplanted by those of coed groups.

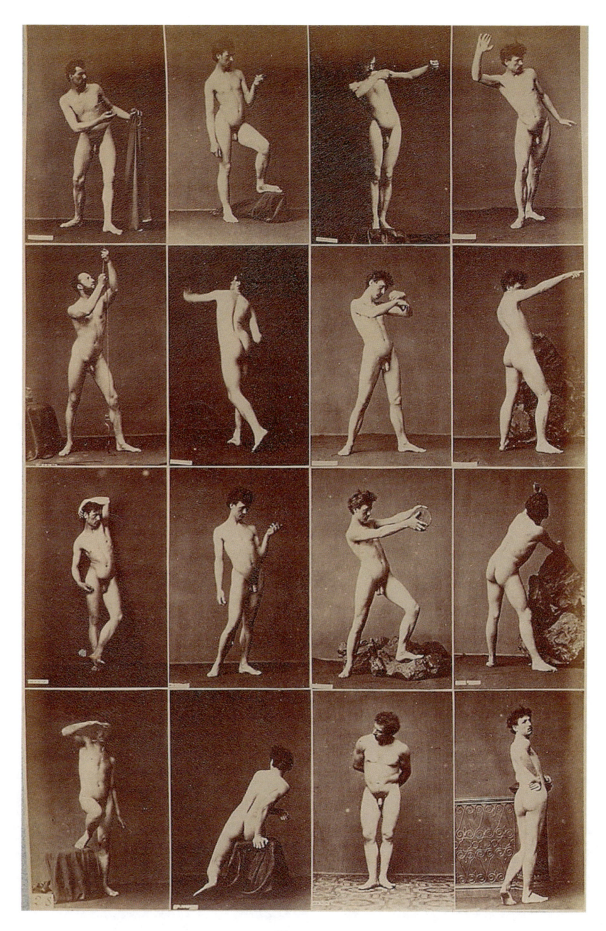

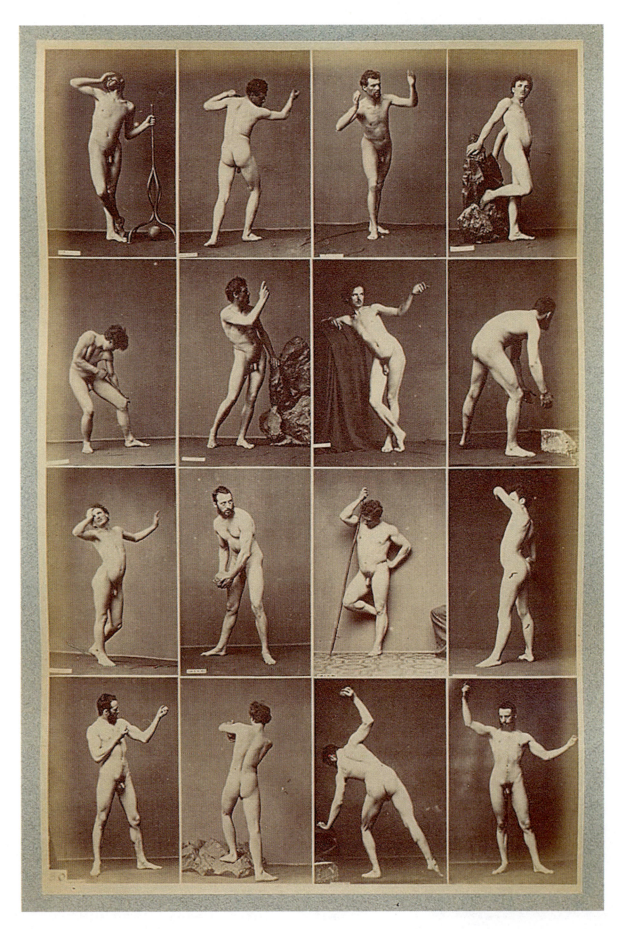

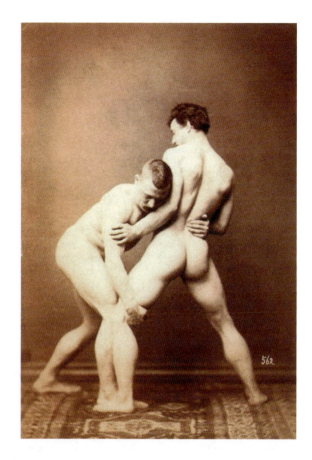

Above, right, left: Igout, *Nude Studies*, c 1870-1880

Photography's debt to historical art is more than imitation or homage; historicism validates new art in the conventional terms of the old. Igout's near selfless role in this supplanting the progress of art has been too long ignored. But search figure drawing or painting classrooms of contemporary art schools and likely there will be found albums of plates of photographs, 'prints albuminous (14 x 20.5 cm), pasted on cardboard box. 16 different stamps per sheet. 624 or thumbnails in total. Format cartons (31 x 23.5 cm), Calavas Brothers, Publishers, 68, rue Lafayette, Paris, (circa 1875).' Igout's images are, for the most part, classical in composition, with a fine use of lighting, props and posing, making these among the most attractive of the late 19th century nude studies.

Though criticized—when even noticed during his time—his albums have been described in sales terms as a 'Total of 39 original plates of French nude photographs featuring men in allegorical poses. Each photographic plate contains 16 photographs mounted on heavy card stock. These studies in the male nude, formed a catalogue of images sold as cheap replacement of life nude models for art students and artists.' After his death in 1881 Louis-Jean Baptiste Igout's contribution through photography to the evolution of subsequent schools could be said to influence photography's making an essential contribution to the development of Surrealist aesthetics by giving pictorial form to the 'gaze of desire'. Metamorphosis, fetishization, gender-switching, scandalization, and hallucination were some of the central themes addressed by Surrealist photographers.

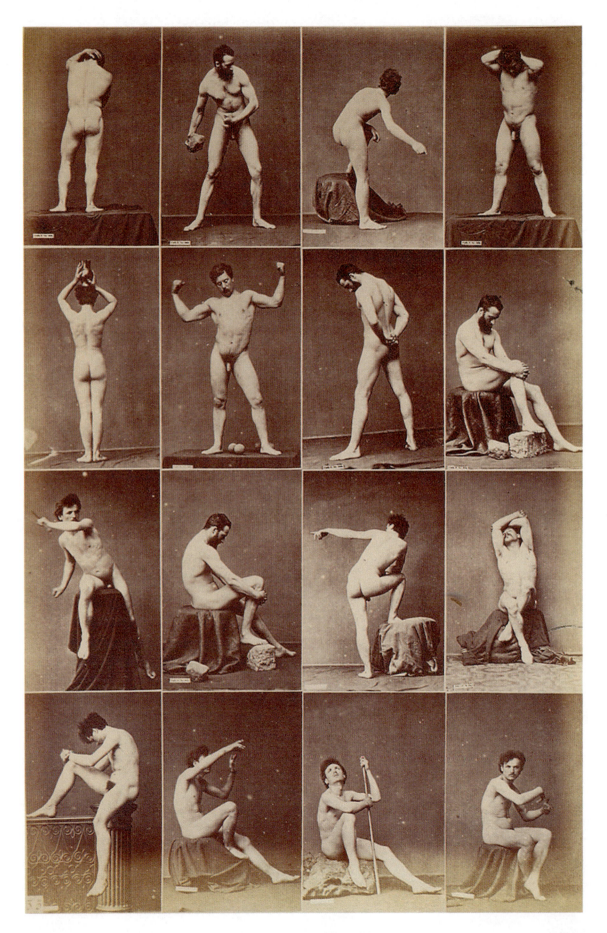

In addition, new possibilities of using the medium were explored in Surrealist novels and journals. Without Igout's contributions, could this have been possible?

Though little is known about Igout's private life, we can probably assume that he was not only an artist with the camera, but also a voyeur who used his instincts to influence the world of art more than he could have imagined. As Alan Griffiths has said on his public website Luminous-Lint, "There are blurred areas between nudity, art, eroticism, obscenity and pornography that are culturally-determined, have changed over time, are difficult to define within laws related to "public morals" and these smudged areas of desire, fascination and guilt are made even more challenging by our own fluctuating attitudes. It is next to impossible to understand the mindsets of photographers and few leave diaries or accounts that provide any indications of how they felt. The surviving material tends to come from law cases and that is rarely a fair judge of the inner motivations of a person. Within nineteenth century there were photographers whose names are linked to Artist studies or Académies which were photographs to assist in drawing and painting where a life model was not available—Louis Igout, Eugène Durieu and Julien Vallou de Villeneuve did nude studies. The vast majority of nineteenth century nude studies were done in France by French photographers."

Perhaps as public interest in the value of his Académies increases, we will discover more about the early years, the training, the private life, and the choice to stay in the shadows Igout preferred. His influence is evident and his contributions post mortem are alarmingly important.

Above: Igout, *Nude Male*, c.1880

Nothing is more dangerous than an idea, when it is the only idea we have. ~Alain

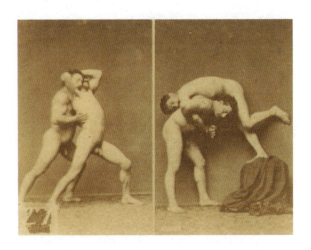

Left and right: Igout, *Nude Studies*, c. 1875–80

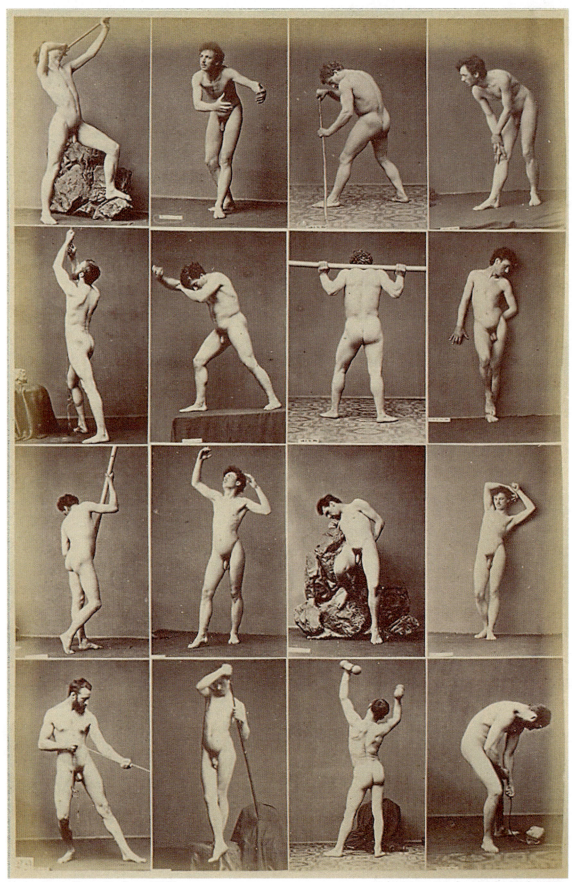

Above: Igout, *Figure Studies*, c. 1875

Right: Igout, *Bacchus-Studie Etude*, 1880

STUDIE ÉTUDE

ALEXEY KLIMOV

Vitruvian Lens: Please introduce yourself.
Alexey Klimov: I am a freelance photographer from Kaliningrad. It's the Russian exclave between Poland and Lithuania on the Baltic Sea.

I have worked as a photographer since 2000. I have no education in the field of photography, I'm self-taught, so to speak. Taking pictures for me is a creative process where my vision of art is revealed.

Several years ago I was a wedding photographer, but now I like to shoot landscapes, buildings, and the male figure. I feel some connection between these three objects—the male body, to me, often looks like a chic relief landscape with rolling hills and ravines. And many of the buildings in a modern style are as sexy as nude body.

V.L.: What do you find fascinating about the male figure as subject?
A.K.: As I see it, the male body is more angular, has a more complex and detailed terrain than the female body. I like how artists Douglas Simonson and Kai Karenin show how men's bodies are composed primarily of chopped forms. For me, visually, it's very exciting.

V.L.: Do you think the male figure will ever be as accepted as the female figure in art?
A.K.: I think that male beauty is less common than the female, because it is more aggressive and physical. Although in recent years the male form often appears in public advertising, I think there is no rivalry between men and women. Now if someone wants a picture of a naked man, he can easily find it.

V.L.: Who are your artistic inspirations?
A.K.: I was always excited and inspired the work of Michelangelo, Leni Riefenstahl, and Bruce Weber. In my opinion, each of these artists was able to create their own artistic and sensual world, which is very close to me in spirit. They have their own vision, their own recognizable and unique style.

Left: Kiimov, *Untitled*, 2012
RightL Kiimov, *Untitled*, 2013

Kiimov, *Untitled*, 2012

Kiimov, *Untitled*, 2014

Above: Kiimov, *Untitled*, 2013
Below: Kiimov, *Untitled*, 2013

Above: Kiimov, *Untitled*, 2012
Right: Kiimov, *Untitled*, 2012

V.L.: When did you first know that you wanted to be a photographer?
A.K.: I think it first started when I saw the famous sculpture of *David* by Michelangelo—I was looking at this flawless male figure and realized that, like Michelangelo, I wanted to capture this *magic* of a male body. For me, the human body is a wonderful gift of nature, and my mission, as a photographer, is to record and preserve this beauty right then and there and then pass it on to others for their appraisal.

When I am doing a male nude, I like to capture a combination of masculine and male power with tenderness, grace, and emotion. My ideal model would be a calm and relaxed superman. He must look like an ancient Greek sculpture, always relaxed, but full of courage and determination. In male figures I like to show the viewer that combination of courage, strength, and delicate grace that can live in the one and same body. I try to be creative with each and every model and to find his own look.

V.L.: Where do you find your models?
A.K.: Most of my models are not professionals. They are ordinary boys, but they all go to the gym to work out and have incredibly beautiful bodies. Basically, I find my models on social networking websites, sometimes on the streets. I love and respect my models. For me they are the best models. I always compliment them on the set, thank them, and express my sincere admiration.

Above: Torso, Greco-Roman sculpture
Left: Kiimov, *Untitled*, 2012

Kiimov, *Untitled*, 2012

V.L.: If you could own just one work of art, which one would it be?

A.K.: In my work, in my life, I've liked the style of minimalism. I love to create effective, but simple images, without unnecessary decorations, concentrating only on the beauty of the model. In the interior of my flat there are no unnecessary details and I carefully select each item I include that is not only practical but also of aesthetic value. So, if I wanted to buy some rare beautiful thing, then perhaps it would be ancient Greek torso—this sort of sculpture certainly would be a great addition to my minimalistic apartment.

V.L.: Who would be your dream model?

A.K.: There are three men with whom I'd like to meet and work, if I could. The problem is that two of them have already died, and the third though alive, but in a fairly advanced age. They would be dancer Rudolf Nureyev, designer Yves Saint Laurent, and actor Alain Delon. In their younger years they looked amazingly cool and stunning. Their images are still attractive and excite me: Rudolf, floating in the air and filled with a wild expression and burning sexuality, Yves—different—shy and hiding behind his glasses, a thin sensual boy. I remember his naked promotional photos for perfume. And Alain attracted me with his sports glamour. I really like the film *La Piscine*, where he probably half of the movie is almost naked and his body is just perfection itself. The images of all three of these people had something rebellious about them. They noticeably stood out from the crowd and I liked it.

Klimov, *Untitled*, 2013

For more information about the artist please visit:
alex-klimov.blogspot.ru
fotoklimov.blogspot.ru

Klimov, *Untitled*, 2013

marc antonio

Vitruvian Lens: Please tell us a bit about yourself.
Marc Antonio: First I'd like to dedicate this interview to my muse, Felix! Second, I actually prefer marc antonio—uncapitalized—even in the titles of my artworks.

I was born and raised in Germany, and am living there as well. My occupational career is fairly unspectacular. While attending school my interest for art was highly pronounced but afterwards disappeared unexplainably for quite a long time. My apprenticeship as a management assistant in data processing was meant to serve as a financial security in the stormy financial waters of Germany. For a while I worked at a job center where I was dealing with people and their existential problems. This experience raised my awareness of them. My relationship to photography commenced suddenly from one day to the next. It was October 2, 1994—I will never forget it. It took just three months till I knew that I wanted to be a photographer and an artist. All the photographic knowledge I master today has been self-taught. Both technical equipment and retouching hardly play a role. The aspects I lay emphasis on are the ideas behind the photos, creativity, as well as the composition of the scene—nothing else matters.

V.L.: Many figurative photographers focus almost exclusively on the female form, why do you include more male figures in your portfolio?
m.a.: The Greeks already had a concrete vision of esthetics and beauty. They frequently found this vision in the depiction of athletic nude males that encouraged them to create perfect statuary. It seems that's just like me. I hold the view that male nude is still under-represented in photography. That's why I've raised the male nude to one of my main subjects.

V.L.: What do you feel is unique about your work?
m.a.: I wouldn't regard my approach as unique. I rather hold the belief that it has become rare to dedicate oneself to a subject with abandon, calmness, time, and respect. Equally significant is the respectful and dignified way of dealing with the model when it comes to nude photography. Many people feel this *in their bones* while looking at my photos. Perhaps it is also about my technical approach since I spend much time getting my ideas realized. This implies that my photographs are created without any retouching.

V.L.: Have you encountered any issues about having the male figure in your work?
m.a.: Unfortunately, there are still quite a lot of galleries which don't have cojones to display the male nude. I have had this experience many times.

V.L.: Do you see a change in the acceptance of the male figure as subject?
m.a.: Thanks to Robert Mapplethorpe, Bruce Weber, and some other good photographers. The subject of the male nude underwent modifications since the nineties. It is definitely a long process of acceptance but from my point of view it is headed in the right direction.

Left: marc antonio, battre et aimer, 2013 (cropped)
Right: marc antonio , uncropped image

Above: marc antonio, *treibgut*, 2011

V.L.: Do you have a humorous experience you can share related to your work, studio, model, or client?
m.a.: One of the most beautiful stories happened to me and my muse Felix at Cap Sounio which is situated 1.5 hours from the Greek capital Athens. On the night of the fifth of December I celebrated my most exceptional birthday by taking photos at this remote location at night. We climbed over a barbed wire fence where Felix ripped his trousers. Finally we took a seat in the center of Poseidon's Temple so that we could enjoy the fantastic view over the sea, the breathtaking appearance of the columns, and the breeze on our faces. At midnight we drank champagne and clinked glassed with each other to appreciate my birthday. The moment was so touching as it was linked with my obsession–photography. I took photos of Felix in the light of Apollo's Muses. The shoot turned out to be tricky because the Greek supply of energy operates according to its own laws. Therefore it denied us the light in the temple several times. We burst into laughter over and over and could hardly believe that the light was switched on and off repeatedly.

V.L.: You have dedicated this interview to your model Felix. Do you believe in muses?
m.a.: Oh yes, of course. Picasso, Dali, and Newton, all of them had had muses. In my mind, Dali's relationship to his muse and wife Gala is particularly impressive. She modeled for him countless times and they loved each other. Some of his masterpieces came into being because of her. I was lucky enough to get to know Felix more than three years ago. From the very first shoot onward we were strongly linked to each other. He understood and appreciated my work, and I came to appreciate him as a model. An affectionate relationship quickly developed which continues to this day and is still inspiring. Felix became an important part of my work. With him together I can go to the limits and even beyond.

marc antonio, *paganini´s traum*, 2012

V.L.: How has your style developed?
m.a.: If any development in my style has happened, it was subtle. From the beginning I felt the urge to create very esthetic and extraordinary works of art. It has to be said that this was not deliberate in regard to both nude photography and still lives. I often desire bringing a storiette or a narrative to life within my photographs. I can only succeed in doing so if I select special settings thoroughly and if I can get the model in partly reckless poses which can even reach the pain barrier. The main thing is that the model, with his pose, fits the setting perfectly. My strongest ambition is that it always looks easy and cushy for the contemplator. Possibly that's what my style is about. Even for my still lives–plenty of times depicting callas or lilies–I work with much effort, especially with respect to the composition. My great love of surrealism influences me a lot in this regard.

V.L.: What subjects you are considering for the future?
m.a.: I would like to head for Xilitla in Mexico to stage a surrealistic scene with a male nude. Hopefully I can collaborate with my muse Felix. I am already wound up to a high pitch. Another subject I would like to deal with is love and sorrow.

V.L.: Tell me something people might not know about you or your work?
m.a.: The viewers of my photographs are often astonished about the fact that I don't do any retouching. I don't even have any editing software. Most of my best nudes were created with my muse Felix. Even though I frequently work collaboratively with him, I am always successful in integrating new aspects in my work and therefore to take, every time, different photographs in unique moments. Furthermore I am willing to spend my last penny on a terrific idea and a good shoot. No pathway is too long or too exhausting for me.

V.L.: Who would be your inspirations?
m.a.: Paramount is Salvador Dali. In my mind, he stands alone in terms of his expertise. Even more, he will always stand alone. Nevertheless, other artists imbue me as well, for instance Man Ray, Helmut Newton, Horst P. Horst, and especially Claude Monet.

V.L.: Where do you find your models?
m.a.: Most of my models I find in my circle of friends. Sometimes I also use online model homepages such as Modelmayhem.com.

V.L.: Tell us about your very first exhibition.
m.a.: My first exhibition was a group show two months after I started taking photos. I just joined a photo club exclusively consisting of girls. The subject was female portraits. As my first shoot was pretty successful, one third of the displayed photos were taken by me. Of course, I was considerably proud of myself. My first solo exhibition was dealing with Venice. In this exhibition my first three photographs were sold.

Six months after my first shoot I had my first solo exhibition titled *Venezia*. I exhibited in a big company. I was fascinated and delighted when three photos found new owners.

marc antonio, *apolls musentempel*, 2011

marc antonio, *der einsame narziss*, 2013

V.L.: When did you know you wanted to be a photographer/artist?

m.a.: On October second, 1994 I took a camera in hand the very first time and cooperated with a female friend who was as pretty as a picture. I exposed three panchromatic films in an old gorgeous factory which now contains an industrial museum. During the shoot and afterwards, an unusual good feeling spread throughout my body. This feeling was close to happiness and inner satisfaction. On December 31, 1994, I went to Venice for the first time. A *million dollar* looking girl accompanied me. I chased her through about half of Venice in January and used more than 10 rolls of film. The experiences, the challenges, and working with a model revealed to me a world of its own which I didn't know up to that time. The work with a model, the attention I gained, as well as the opportunity to express myself in a different way, filled me with great enthusiasm and fascination. I had the feeling of burning ambition in my body. Because of these experiences in Venice I knew that I wanted to be a photographer and an artist.

V.L.: Have you ever been brought to tears in front of a work of art?

m.a.: It happened more than once to me. Full of expectations and pleasant anticipation, I visited a big exhibition of surrealists in the Centre George Pompidou in Paris in 1996. There were many works by Salvador Dali. I was already overcome with joy when entering the exhibition. The abundance of exhibits, the play of colors, and the variety—everything was stunning. I was enamored by Salvador Dali's paintings. I was left in disbelief of the breath-taking, creative abundance he provided us, with insights into his world. When I stood in front of *Swans Reflecting Elephants*, teardrops were rolling down my face and I didn't feel ashamed of myself at all. I guess I was overwhelmed with emotion due to the creativity, the prowess and the expertise of this painting.

marc antonio, *cascata III*, 2011 (uncropped cover image)

V.L.: What subject is the most challenging for you as an artist to capture?
m.a.: On the one hand I would regard my nudes as the most challenging to capture and on the other hand, still lives. The nude shoots often take place in extraordinary settings. A lot of times these are popular places which are heavily frequented—a church at Lake Garda, the Oracle of Delphi, or the Poseidon Temple at Cap Sounio, to name but a few. To take nude photographs at these places, good and thorough preparation is required as well as a good feeling for timing. I never ask for permission. Working together with my muse Felix often makes it much easier. Meanwhile we are a well-established team. My still lives—mostly surrealistically staged—are very time-consuming in the composition and often fragile. That's why I need to show great patience and endurance.

marc antonio, *antagonism*, 2014

V.L.: If you could own just one work of art, which one would it be? Pretend money is not an issue.
m.a.: It would be *Water Lilies* from 1906, by Claude Monet. I can get completely immersed in that painting for hours on end lingering over dreams of a different world.

V.L.: Do you collect art? If so, what do you collect?
m.a.: Honestly, I am my biggest collector... no, all joking aside, I possess a beautiful photograph by Henning von Berg and two large-sized paintings by a lesser-known painter.

marc antonio, *if he had wings V*, 2014

marc antonio, *apolls musen* II, 2011

marc antonio, *green*, 2011

For more information about the artist, visit:
www.marcantonio-photografien.de
www.tinyurl.com/lwdtnoc

To see his work in person, please visit
Gallery Nieser in Stuttgart
www.galerie-nieser.de

Federico, *Two Faces*, 2014

UMBERTO FEDERICO

Vitruvian Lens: Please introduce yourself.
Umberto Federico: I was born in Germany and I currently live close to Munich. My dad is Italian—hence an Italian name—and my mother is from Poland.

I'm not a professional photographer and I never really studied photography. I basically started by teaching myself through the various online channels that are available nowadays. I began shooting male nudes only two years ago as I started developing an interest in working with people instead of shooting only landscapes or cityscapes. The first attempts turned out pretty good and so I started to experiment a lot and push myself forward. I tried to come up with new ideas and concepts and with every new session, I improved my photography as well as my editing skills.

As a gay photographer who takes photos of mostly nude males, it is difficult to position yourself in a place where people don't see you as just another guy who takes pictures of young men for his own pleasure. I learned that you can only do that if your photos are respectfully done, never pornographic, and always with style and beauty.

V.L.: Many figurative photographers focus almost exclusively on the female form, why do you include more male figures in your portfolio?
U.F.: I shoot only men because I love the male body and its shapes. The male figure is often a symbol of strength, dominance—the strong one that never shows emotions or weakness. I want to show the soft side instead: the subtle, sensual, emotive side—the vulnerable side.

Right: Federico, *Torn*, 2014

Federico, *Breath*, 2013

V.L.: What is it about your work or approach that you feel is most unique?
U.F.: I don't see the model as an object. I always try to get a feel for his personality and use that to come up with my concepts. I don't give many directions while shooting—I'd rather observe and tell the model to hold a pose or an expression. I love the use of symbolism in my photographs. The eyes of a person to me are the most fascinating and most important things.

V.L.: Are there subjects you are considering for future works you can share?
U.F.: I want to start shooting more conceptual art as seen in my photo *Two Faces* and I am currently working on some photos that fit into that genre. Something specific I'm going to try is incorporating the use of ropes—bondage—into my upcoming shoots—not in a erotic or sexual way, but more as an aesthetic element in the photo.

V.L.: How do you feel when your work pops up on social websites like Tumblr or Pinterest?
U.F.: I feel great because I mostly get positive feedback and I see that people actually understand what I'm trying to express. I also enjoy talking to other photographers and sharing ideas, techniques, experiences, as well as getting feedback on my work.

V.L.: Who would be your inspirations as an artist?
U.F.: One of the photographers I admire the most is Peter Lik for his breathtaking analog landscapes and nature shots. Another artist I really like is Rob Woodcox. His conceptual art is simply amazing and I'm impressed by his ideas and the effort he puts into his sets.

Federico, *Sunk*, 2014

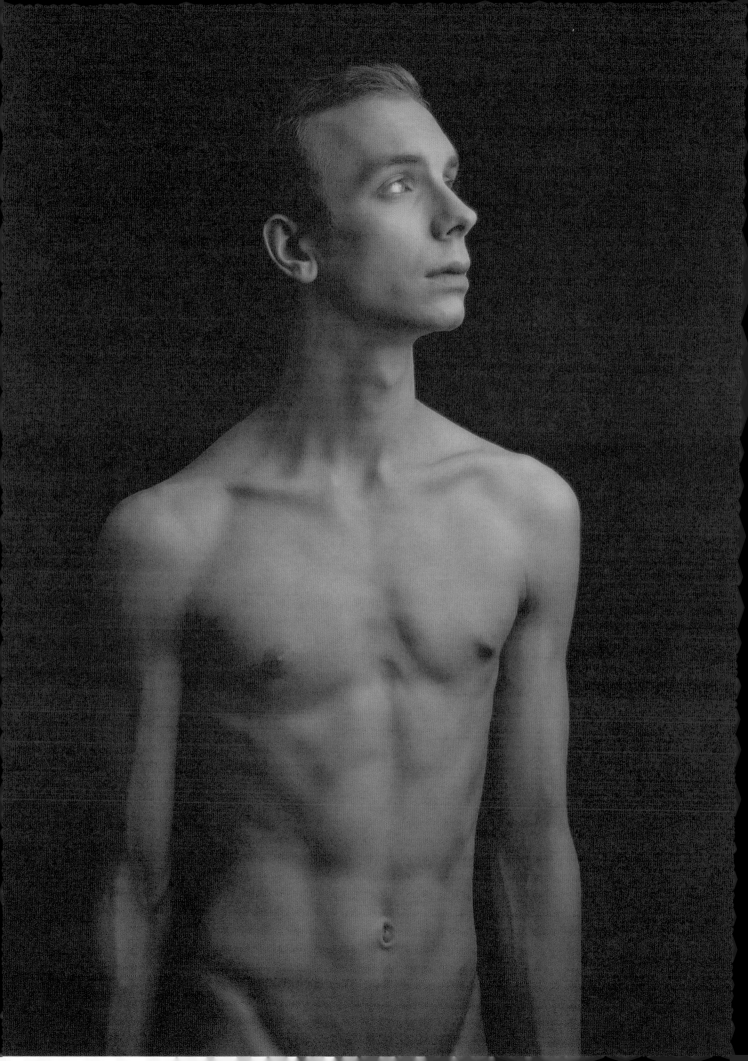

Left: Federico, *Ready*, 2014

Above: Federico, *Floating World*, 2013

V.L.: How has your style developed?
U.F.: Well I guess in the beginning I didn't think much about what to shoot and how to edit. I tried to find a model and we then started to shoot with no specific goal. Then in post production I just tried some presets and the ones that looked the best became the one that the photo ended up with.

Today I plan my shoots in advance and I know my gear, lighting concepts, my way of editing, and the topics I want to get through. I would say that my photos are more expressive and are more consistent in terms of quality and style.

V.L.: Tell me something people might not know about you or your work?
U.F.: Well—I am a singer/songwriter and photography really happened by accident. I got my first DSLR camera to shoot music videos for YouTube. Since I had one, I started playing around with it and so I got into the whole photography subject. Today I rarely travel without my camera and I mostly have it at hand even if I don't have anything planned.

V.L.: Where do you find your models?
U.F.: I mostly find them online. I am pretty picky about the selection of a model and so it's not always easy to find someone to work with. One time it was the other way around—I got an e-mail from a guy who had heard of me through a friend and after checking out my work, he decided to contact me. He wrote a really nice long email saying that he would love to be photographed by me. The funny thing was that he wrote in English and you could tell that English wasn't his mother tongue. I replied to him and asked him why he didn't write in German. He just said that since my website was in English, he thought I couldn't speak German. That was really funny. We met a couple of days later and I shot some beautiful photos.

Above: Federico, *Line Of Passion*, 2014

Below: Federico, *Shame*, 2013

Federico, *Stripes*, 2013

V.L.: Tell us about your very first exhibition.
U.F.: My first exhibition was here in Munich and I got a ton of great reviews and feedback. I didn't showcase my male photos though—it was a mixed exhibition with twelve artists along with painters and sculptors. I displayed two urban shots which got a lot of attention. One was the skyline of Shanghai and the other one was an aerial shot of New Delhi's airport right after sunrise. I spent the whole evening talking to guests about my travels and how I pick my shots. The woman who organized the exhibition and who is in charge of the art department at the bank it all happened at bought one of my photographs because she was blown away by it.

V.L.: When did you know you wanted to be a photographer/artist?
U.F.: I wanted to become a photographer when I started to travel the world. I always wanted to bring something home with me. Something you cannot buy—a moment—a feeling. That's when I started taking pictures. In the beginning I only had a point and shoot camera.

V.L.: Are you a full time photographer?
U.F.: I do have a main job—photography is something I only do besides that. I am a flight attendant which gives me the opportunity to travel the world, and I think I try to cherish each and every trip by always going out and shooting the beautiful sights I encounter.

V.L.: If you could own just one work of art, which one would it be? Pretend money is not an issue.
U.F.: *Antelope Cathedral* by Peter Lik. I love it!
V.L.: I recommend to both you and our readers who enjoy photography to visit Antelope Canyon. It is a stunning natural formation near the Grand Canyon.

Federico, *Luminosity*, 2013

V.L.: What artwork or artist impresses you?
U.F.: There have been pieces of art that took my breath away or impressed me a lot. The work of Kevin Rossatty is such an example. I love his work and the colors and how he shoots photos of himself in a way I haven't seen before.

V.L.: What subject is the most challenging for you as an artist to capture?
U.F.: True emotion, a feeling. When I come up with my concepts, I always have a feeling in mind. I want to express joy, sadness, determination, or whatever other feeling might fit–all through one single shot.

It's not always easy to get the model to actually feel that way and show it to the camera, but I think I've captured some good expressions and people told me that they really like what my photos express.

V.L.: Do you collect art? If so, what do you collect?
U.F.: I don't, but I want to start collecting. And I think it's gonna be male art.

V.L.: If you could wave a magic wand and anyone in the world would appear to be your next male model, who would that dream model be?
U.F.: Robert Sheehan from the TV Series *Misfits*. I adore his eyes and I love the curly hair and lean body he has. I think he would be a fun guy to work with.

For more information about the artist, please visit:
www.umbertofederico.de

Federico, *The Essence*, 2014

VINTAGE COLLECTION

The internet and sites like Tumblr, Pinterest, and even Facebook have become a place to find and share all kinds of things of interest. We find antiques, books, collectibles, even sources for vintage images of the male figure. Though Von Gloeden and others are well known, these sites have become the virtual museums to collections that do not exist in a physical form. Certainly some museums have works in their collections, but are often reluctant to show them on a regular basis. Many lie in the hands of collectors, and may never see the light of day. We are aware of many collections found by the families of deceased collectors or artists, thrown away or even burned. The names of the artists for many of the images we present here may be lost for all time.

As we at *Vitruvian Lens* attempt to feature artists of the male figure, we tie them to the traditions of nineteenth century photography, and even some twentieth century examples. What an artist does today is influenced by their predecessors. We'd argue that nothing is totally new or unique. Photographers of today are influenced by their peers, who were influenced by their previous generations, and so on. Even though we can date the beginnings of modern photography to the mid 1800s, even these artists were influenced by the painters and sculptors before them.

Turkish Strongmen, Unattributed

Left: Portrait of F Holland Day with Male Nude Clarence H White 1902 Platinum print

Unattributed vintage image

Thomas Eakins, *Horse and Rider*, 1892 Hirshhorn Museum Collection

 As we search out photographers there are specific things we look for. We seek out those who are tied to the classical masters through subject or approach. We look for clarity of vision and message. We seek out those with singular and unique approach to the male figure. You have no doubt noticed that a large portion of the artists we have featured here and in previous editions are often self taught. I'd argue that a good eye for photography is something that cannot be fully taught, but is innate to the artist.

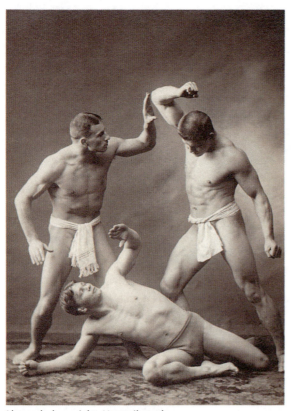

Above, below, right: Unattributed.

Below: Painting class at l'Académie des Beaux Arts

Above, below, right: Unattributed.

Below: Portrait of Gustav Frištenský from Prague

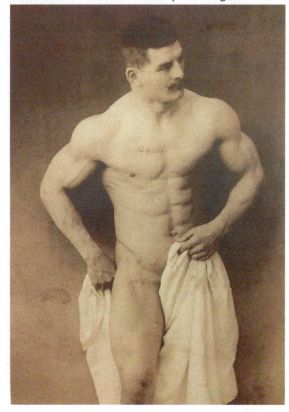

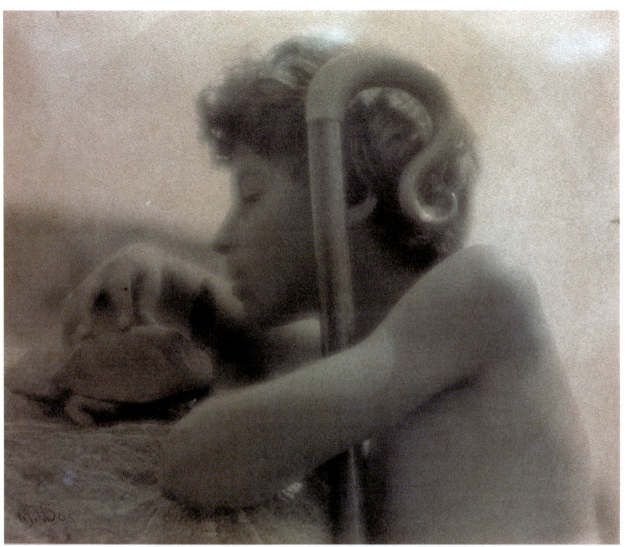

Right: *Young Male Nude Seated on Leopard Skin*, Guglielmo Plüshow, c.1890 Albumen silver print
Above: *Male with Shepherd's Crook and Turtle*, F. Holland Day, 1905

As we review an artist's portfolio, we look for the qualities I mentioned. We care more for the work than the pedigree of the artist. We have featured an artist who was just sixteen years of age, and those in their golden years. We have featured artists who are gay, who are straight, men and women, young and old. Quality, we hope, has come through in our curatorial selections. We know what we like, and that is what we choose to publish.

Though a search of male photography may yield vast results, the quality or originality we speak of is often lacking. So too is the connection to classical modes that resonate with dignity, honor, beauty, and purpose. So often the field of male photography is focused on vapid images meant to titillate or provide masturbatory material—so little of it is *artful*.

It is for this reason we have waited to produce this series of books. You may know we also produce *The Art of Man*, dedicated to the male figure in the fine arts of painting, drawing, and sculpture. As we built that series we kept finding, once in a while, photographers that

Above: Unattributed   Below: Japanese Wrestlers

Unattributed Image

Nude with Trumpet, Fred Holland Day, 1897

truly used their media to create what we see as *fine art*. We noted these artists, followed them via their websites, and in 2013 began to approach them one by one.

They too saw the disparity within their own field, and embraced our mission and message. We are so happy to give them a place to speak to you, our dear reader, and share their stories. We support them through our publications, and you support them through the purchase of this book, and we hope you have reached out to the artists that have grabbed your attention and supported them with a purchase.

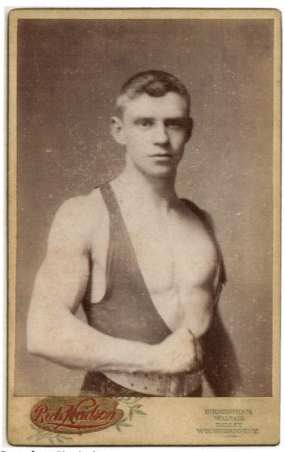
Boxer from Birmingham

Guglielmo Plüschow

Orpheus, 1907, by F. Holland Day

3 Viro Brothers

Above: Cvičitelský Sokol Prague choir from 1876

Below: Unattributed

DIRECTORY:

Artists from Edition 6

Guy Yechiely
facebook.com/guyyechielyart
www.guyyechiely.com
Email: Guytlv@gmail.com

Karl Lakolak
www.lakolak.info

Alexey Klimov
alex-klimov.blogspot.ru
fotoklimov.blogspot.ru

marc antonio
www.marcantonio-photografien.de
www.tinyurl.com/lwdtnoc
www.galerie-nieser.de

Umberto Federico
www.umbertofederico.de

Artists from Edition 5

Empyrean Photography
André DeLoach
empyreanphotography.foliodrop.com

Aurelio Monge
aureliomonge.prosite.com
www.flickr.com/photos/mgartstudio
www.facebook.com/aureliomonGe

Joan Alsina
www.joanalsina.com

Marc Kiska
www.marckiska.com
contact@marckiska.com

West Phillips
facebook.com/westphillipsphoto
instagram: west_phillips

Richard Stabbert
www.createspace.com/4504319
www.rstabbert.com

Artists from Edition 4

Antonio Salazar
www.eccehomo.mx
www.tinyurl.com/kz4cuua

Daniel Nassoy
http://danielnassoy.com
http://jeveuxmonportrait.com
http://myportraitinparis.com
http://menofmydreams.com

Eric Shultis
www.eshultis.com

Henning von Berg
www.Henning-von-Berg.com
blurb.com/b/1777508-men-pure

James Bidgood
ClampArt
www.clampart.com

Michael Bilotta
www.michaelbilotta.com
Flickr.com/photos/shibbopics
www.tinyurl.com/kbuqrkm

Artists from Edition 3

Collin McAdoo
www.tinyurl.com/KNQW942

David Vance
www.davidvanceprints.com
www.davidvance.com

DDiArte
http://1x.com/artist/63782
www.olhares.com/ddiarte
facebook.com/ddiarte

Enzo Truppo
http://tinyurl.com/Ln7hmsu
http://tinyurl.com/mt88yqm

Frank Aron Gårdsø
http://500px.com/frankenstyle
www.wix.com/fr3575/studiotrolliord

Michel Gelin
www.michelgelin.com

Artists from Edition 2

Jim Ferringer
www.modelmayhem.com/1404482
www.redbubble.com/people/jimm150

J.D. Dragan
www.jddragan.com

Gregg Friedberg
gefriedberg@gmail.com
gfriedberg.deviantart.com

Adi Nes
Jack Shainman Gallery, NYC
www.jackshainman.com

Adam Collier Noel
www.adamcolliernoel.com
www.lymaneyerart.com

Aernout Overbeeke
www.aernoutoverbeeke.com

Heitor Magno
www.flickr.com/heitorm

Michel Guillaume
www.michelguillaume.fr
www.shootingmode.com.

Artists from Edition 1

Nectario Karolos Papazacharias
www.nectariopapazacharias.com

Ed Freeman
www.edfreeman.com

David Jarrett
www.davidjarrett-photography.com

Ren Hang
www.renhang.org

Max Woltman
www.maxwoltman.com

E. Gibbons
www.firehousegallery.com/info.htm
www.lymaneyerart.com

Dianora Niccolini
www.dianoraniccolini.com

Recommended Galleries

Lyman-Eyer Gallery
Provincetown, MA
www. lymaneyerart.com

Leslie + Lohman Museum of Gay
and Lesbian Art, Manhattan, NY
www.leslielohman.org

PHD Gallery
St. Louis, MO
www.phdstl.com

Lizardi/Harp Gallery
Pasadena CA
626-791-8123

Galerie Mooi-Man
Groningen, Netherlands
www.mooi-man.NL

Recommended Websites

TheArtOfMan.net

PowerfullyBeautiful.com

100ArtistsBook.com

100ArtistsBook.tumblr.com

www.sachetmixte.com

www.VitruvianLens.com

www.BigKugels.com

Other Books We Publish

Powerfully Beautiful
www.createspace.com/3382894

365 Art Quotes
www.createspace.com/3904538

100 Artists of the Male Figure
www.100ArtistsBook.com

The Art Of Man
www.TheArtOfMan.net

Provincetown Memories
www.createspace.com/4504319

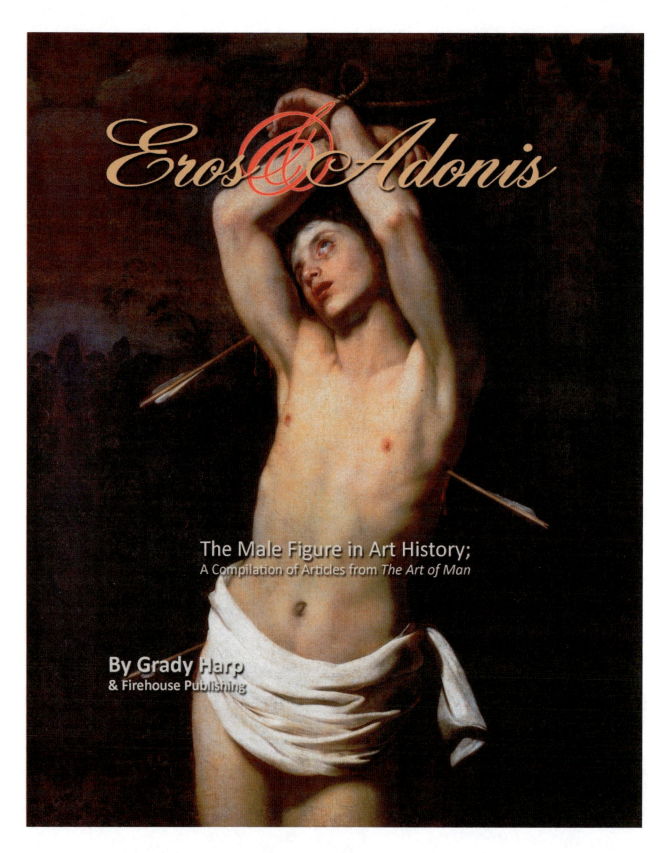

The classical male figure in art history, available in soft cover,
and online at www.TheArtOfMan.net

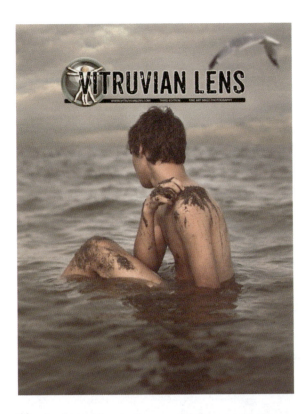

Vitruvian Lens strives to discover and showcase photographers with a fine art approach to the male figure. We offer a non-erotic option to those who love figurative art with an international point of view with interviews that explore their thought processes, choices, and struggles in a way no book does. www.VitruvianLens.com

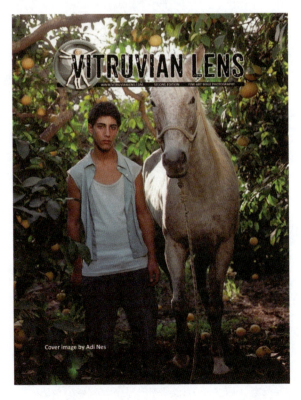

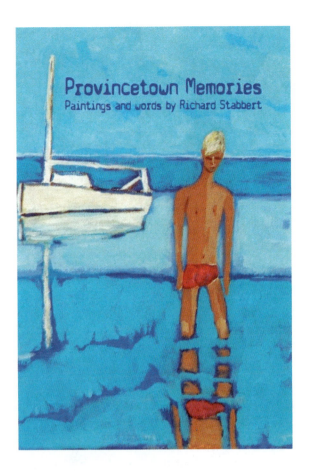

Richard Stabbert is a self-taught painter. He documents the people in his life, both past and present, referencing them, the objects around him, and his love of the beach. All of his images are tied together by a sensuality of brushstroke. He limits his palette to evoke spare, almost graphic forms, as color in itself and line that have a resonance and symbolism for Stabbert.

Picasso once said, *"It took me four years to paint like Raphael, but a lifetime to paint like a child."*

Stabbert is one who embraces the simplicity of his style and approaches his work with passion and enthusiasm. We see his words and works through the eyes of adolescent self-discovery and passion. Richard describes young love, from first flirt to first love, and everything in-between, most often centered here, in the artist colony of Provincetown, Massachusetts. The Newest collection from the publishers of *The Art of Man*.

www.createspace.com/4504319

100 Artists of the Male Figure
A Contemporary Anthology of Painting, Drawing, and Sculpture

E. Gibbons
Introduction by Grady Harp

Info: www.100ArtistsBook.com

Schiffer

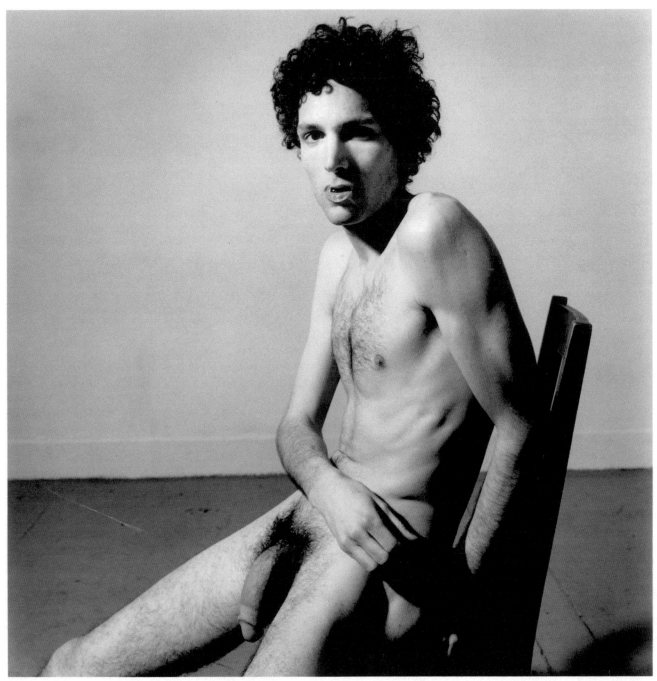

Peter Hujar, *Nude Blowing Spit Bubbles*, 1980, Vintage silver gelatin print, 14.625 x 14.688 in. Gift of the Peter Hujar Archive. Collection of Leslie-Lohman Museum

Leslie + Lohman museum of Gay and Lesbian Art

26 Wooster Street
New York, NY 10013
Tuesday-Sunday: 12-6
Thursday: 12-8
LeslieLohman.org

More info about Vitruvian Lens, back issues, submissions, and more can be found at: VitruvianLens.com

No assumptions should be made about the gender or sexuality of the artists. Though all of the artists dedicate a significant portion of their portfolio to the classical male form, they are equally adept in other subjects as well.

We always seek artists who dedicate 50% or more of their portfolio to the male figure and promote those artists at no cost here. Vitruvian Lens also actively seeks vintage images for future publications. Information about being featured in a future edition, sharing your collection, and more can be found on our website: www.VitruvianLens.com

We thank you for your purchase, reviews, and support.